CASTAWAYS

Barbara Brooks

ISBN: 978-0-578-92849-4

INTRODUCTION

The very *last time* I was with my **Dad**, was on a Sunday in the hospital in Hesston, Ks.

He took his walker and his Bible, and we walked down to the hospital chapel.

He turned to **John 21** *in his* **Bible** and started reading. He stopped at v.18 & 19 and asked me to read!

"I assure you, most solemnly I tell you, when you were young, you girded yourself, put on your own belt, and you walked about wherever you pleased to go. But when you grow old you will stretch out your hands and someone else will put a girdle around you and carry you where you do not wish to go. He said this to indicate by what kind of death Peter would glorify God. And after this He said to him, Follow Me!

Suddenly, I started to cry, but did not know why!

Reaching out to ***you*** as you are reading and listening, with great ***understanding, compassion,*** reaching into parts of your life that have been painful, and giving you right now, that **hope** that no one around you has ever given you, that life can be **restored!**

Dedicating this first book to the memory of my Dad **Pastor Carl Brooks Jr.,**

1927-1998

CONTENTS

Chapter 1

Mentorship

At age 12, on a Saturday night, watching Billy Graham, I received Jesus as my Lord and Savior!

The next Sunday my dad baptized me, starting the journey by knowing more about Jesus.

As a *pastor's kid*, I had a problem with distinguishing my dad, from being my pastor.

I became *rebellious,* and *very self-centered.*

In my late 20s, my mother, **Betty,** a pastor's wife, took an *overdose* of prescription pills after leaving *behind a suicide* note!

I was always taught God was in control. I immediately blamed everyone, but most of all, I became *angry at*

God.

I lifted my hand in anger to God, saying, "*I want no part of you!*"

I carried that *hurt and pain* deep into my 40s.

In that season of my life, I was falling apart. My first mentor, Rose, started praying for me; she was a friend of mine, also a preacher's kid, in my teenage years!

She had come from the same religion I had grown up in, and was familiar with my background.

I will never forget the day when she went with me to my *mother's grave, me carrying* a *picture* of my mom. As I sat there, she began praying for me. My emotions were totally *numb,* looking at Mom's picture.

Rose looked at me with the first of several questions:

"What did she do?" Things started pouring out of my mouth like an erupting volcano, with an odor!

She asked me a second question:

"How did it make you feel?" Again, it was like vomit with **an** odor coming out of me.

She asked me the third question, "**What has it cost you?**" Like a flood of anger, I pounded the ground on her grave.

Then and only then, did *true forgiveness* come!

I lay there, asking **God** to forgive me for I had become angry at Him as if He *was the problem.*

God is in control of His plan to redeem man!

However, **God** has given *man* the freedom to choose.

God *honors* His decision to give mankind the *will to choose.*

He will allow us to make a *mess* of our lives, not because that is *His will,* and not because that is what *He* desires for us, but because *He* decided to *allow us to choose.*

In the Old Testament, **God** gave the people of Israel a choice: life or death, the blessing, or the curse.

God's desire for us is that we make the right decisions and right choices.

How can I blame **God** for the death of my mother, when **He was not the problem!**

I realized then, if I believed God caused the problem, how can I see Him as my solution?

My *belief system* changed, as the **Word of God** became life to me. I repented of believing Satan's lies and forgave myself so I would not carry this guilt into my future.

James 1:14-15: "*But every man is tempted when he is drawn away of his lust and enticed. Then when lust hath conceived, it bringeth forth sin, and sin, when it is finished, bringeth forth death.*"

I realized I could not do anything for Mom; she had made her choice!

In That Moment, praying: "Father God, do not let her death be in vain!"

I had no idea, at that time, how my lifestyle would change, as I followed in my mother's career footsteps, in nursing. As I later surrendered to **God's** will, doors started opening for me, jobs in home health care as a caregiver.

I have now had a lifetime of blessings and miracles, with private duty and with various companies.

As I got up from Mom's grave, it was like loads of bricks I had been carrying for years, simply *slid off.*

I rested in Rose's home for hours recovering, as I listened to soft praise music, filling up my soul and mind; where there was pain, there was now peace!

The Word of God became very real to me in, John 11:35: "JESUS WEPT."

My question was: Why did ***Jesus*** *weep?*

For there is no record of weeping like this at the cross, for then He asked the "Father to forgive them for they know not what they do." Luke: 23:34

Jesus was feeling the pain of those that loved Lazarus!

Martha had told Jesus, what she thought he did,
and how it made her feel and what it had cost her.

What did **Jesus** say? Verse 39: "Take the stone away."

"But Lord there will be an odor, for it has been 4 days."

That day when I was at my mother's grave,
I chose to take the stone away!

Holy Spirit, right now, I send the Word of God into *each person* that is reading or listening to this, going into their *dying place*, where there is *deep pain, anger, and hurt.*

Jesus has wept for you!

I pray that, Father God, You will send an anointed servant of God into their lives to help take *away their stone*, for the anointing will break the yoke that is holding them down. In Jesus Name!

Chapter 2

Loved Back to God

Love is like a strong ocean current. I encounter that kind of love with God daily. He turned my pain into His greater purpose.

I began attending weekly classes at Life Skills International, founded by Paul and Judy Hegstrom's Domestic Abuse Recovery Program.

Having a hunger for truth, I started learning what I did not know. 1 Tim: 2:4: "Who will have all men to be saved, and to come unto the knowledge of the truth."

I was given a Living Bible that I could not put down. This started my journey back to the **Word of God.**

Pro 4:7: "Wisdom is the principal thing, therefore, get Wisdom, and with all thy getting, get understanding."

In this season of my life Paul Hegstrom, through the classes, became my *mentor!*

When ***God*** **wanted to bless me,** *He put a person in my life, but when Satan wanted to destroy me, he also put a person in my life. Mentorship helped me know the difference.*

Soul-Ties: *How can a soul-tie start?*

Eph. 6:12: "*For we wrestle not against flesh and blood, but against principalities, against power, against the rulers of the darkness of this world, against spiritual wickedness in high places.*"

While experiencing a demonic soul-tie, my communication in hearing shut down because of believing wrong words that were said to me. The only open channels of communication were through vision and touch.

Satan put someone in my life that fed on these open channels, with lust, anger, hopelessness, believing that this was love. Once I started believing these lies, the cord of feeding back and forth from his open channels to mine, began. No matter how far away I traveled or tried to leave the relationship, I always returned.

Why should I cut and break a soul-tie?

Matt. 22:37: *"Jesus said unto him, thou shall love the Lord Thy God with all thy heart, and with all thy soul, and with all thy mind."*

How to break a soul-tie?

I repented of believing Satan's lies, going to the cross of Jesus, breaking, and cutting the soul-tie that was attached to me.

Eph: 6:17: "And take the helmet of salvation and the sword of the spirit, which is the Word of God."

There was a reaction of anger when I broke and cut the soul-tie cord, for there was nothing that could be attached to me any longer. The Blood of Jesus covered and healed where it had been attached.

In a desperate season, believing those lies, almost *ended my life.* One morning I rode my bicycle down to a cove at the Mississippi River.

I was angry, and furious, inside. I thought I had dug my hole so deep, even God *could not reach or help me.*

I saw a boat by the bridge with divers looking for a person that had jumped earlier that day. Because of the strength of the current, they did not find the body.

I really did not want that to happen to me. So, I just sat there at the riverside, looking at how powerful the water currents were.

All I could remember was, "**God created the earth!" Gen 1:1**

I desperately *cried* out: "**God,** You made this river; w**ill you help me**"! A peace came over me that I had not known before, and I backed away from the river. K*nowing I had just had an encounter with* ***God!***

In a delicate healing season of breaking soul-ties, I received a letter in the mail, from the person I had broken the soul-tie with!

My mentor, Rose, said, "I will read it if you want, and if there are any 911 items, I will let you know. If not, I will put it in the file for your reading it at another time."

Weeks passed and as we were visiting, Rose went to get the file, and handed me the letter with two highlighters, one for any truth I found, and the other highlighter for any lies.

I started reading and highlighting, finding out the page was full of lies and only *one sentence* at the bottom was a truth!

Rev 12:11: "And they have overcome him by means of the blood of the Lamb and by the utterance of their testimony."

John 8:32: "*And ye shall know the truth, and the truth shall make you free.*"

Wisdom Key: **GET YOUR STUFF TOGETHER, BEFORE YOUR STUFF GETS YOU!!!!**

Chapter 3

Wounded Inner child

I continued to attend Family Life Skills' weekly classes. I started having dreams of the past that I did not understand. I went into prayer, asking **God** to reveal the truth.

Looking at different pictures of my childhood, this one picture of my grandfather, a pastor, stood out.

I prayed, "God, keep my grandma, Hellen, *alive until I find out the truth, for she was the only one that could help me with this childhood memory.*" *In Jesus Name!*

I went to visit my grandma at the nursing home, and asked her, "*Was I ever with Grandpa by myself?*" She said, "Yes."

Weeks went by and I had another visit with her, and we went out to a restaurant.

I knew something was wrong. She hung her head and said, that she had found out through talking to a family member over the phone, that the *same thing that happened to me, happened to another family member.*

Which matched up with the *dreams* I had,
that I had never shared with anyone.

I went into the restroom, shocked, and started to cry, trying to keep myself together while at the restaurant.

I knew, from family comments, what had
happened to the other family member.

That next Sunday, I went to chapel with Rose,
and as we went into worship, I started crying
uncontrollably on the floor. *I felt so dirty and broken!*

How could God love me now?

In that little chapel, is where **Jesus**
met me, right where I was!

As I was deeply broken, my inner
child was wounded and afraid! **Jesus's**
love touched me that moment, as
I reached to Him as a child!

Mark 10:14: "Suffer the little children to come unto me, and forbid them not, for of such is the kingdom of God."

I continued to go to chapel each Sunday,
to receive more from ***God's Word!***

Weeks later I received a phone
call that my *grandma* had a stroke
and was not expected to live.

I stayed at her bedside for 3 days. At one point
I asked, "Grandma, if you can hear me just,
please squeeze my hand," and *she did!*

As I prayed, I could tell that she was upset,
for it was *kept from her* what had happened
to me as a child. I told her, that *I forgave
her, as I had asked for forgiveness too.*

I slept in her chair, with the continuing praise
music playing, "**In His Presence.**"

When I opened my eyes from my sleep, Grandma's **paralyzed arm was raised, with eyes wide open, looking up.**

Then she took her last breath, and
then I knew she was in **Heaven.**

I sat there, thanking **God** for this special time,
I had with her!

Chapter 4

Castaway

My whole foundation had been shaken, as I searched for a church. Each one believed some of the Bible but did not believe *all* of it!

I became a *Castaway* from the Body of Christ, as I knew it at that time!

I became *terribly angry*, and I raised my hand in frustration to **God**!

Saying, "**I will never go back to church again!**" I did not attend church for a long time after that.

Years later, in Texas, I was invited to go to a conference at a local church, so I agreed.

The guest speaker stopped the service and asked for "All the preachers' kids to **stand up**." So, I did!

He started speaking as if he knew my life!

He spoke, "*There is someone here that has a deaf and dumb spirit.*"

As he started praying; my spiritual ears opened, and my physical *ears* popped. I became weak and shaken, under the power of **God!**

I had to put cotton in my physical ears for days, for any sounds would bother me.

I noticed that there was a difference in reading my Bible. I had more *understanding* of what I was reading.

Chapter 5

Baptism of the Holy Spirit

Rose invited me to go to a church that they started attending. Knowing my background issues, she spoke, "I *will sit with you and will not let anything harm you.*" So, I went.

As the church service began, the music was so different from what I had ever heard. People started praising in a way I had never experienced before.

I asked her: "What are they happy about?" The pastor began to speak on the P*ower of the Holy Spirit.*

This was something I had never heard. He said,
"You need the power of the Holy Spirit."

Eph: 6:18: "*Praying always with all prayer and supplication in the spirit.*"

Rose and I looked at each other, and *we both* went forward to receive the baptism of the Holy Spirit.

As the women started praying for me, I remember them saying: "A*ll denotational walls must come down, in Jesus' Name!*"

I started to cry! I wanted more of **God!**

I received the *gift* of the Holy Spirit with the heavenly language, with a joy and peace that I had never known before.

Luke 11:13: "If ye then, being evil, know how to give good gifts unto your children, how much more shall your heavenly Father give the Holy Spirit to them that ask Him."

As I started the journey, getting to know the Holy Spirit as a "person" that walked beside me. I never felt alone anymore.

Anytime I felt my inner child being afraid or in need, the Holy Spirit was always there.

Chapter 6

Repeating

Weeks went by and I saw changes in the way I talked, for I was told that "I *cussed* like a sailor!"

I regularly attended church with Rose. One Sunday the pastor stated, "D*o not take my word for it; study this in your own* ***Bible,"*** for that was the *first* time I had ever heard someone say I did not have to believe them!!

That gave me a hunger for Godly wisdom and decrement.

As I, daily, meditated on my **Bible**, I saw
things I had never known, convinced
of lies that I had believed for years!

Finding the truth, brought me to my
knees as I spent time grieving.

Heb 4:15: "For we have not a high priest which cannot be touched with the feeling of our infirmities but was in all points tempted, like as we are, yet without sin."

One of the toughest class assignments I had, was to examine past religious teachings, and ask myself: "**Is this the truth?**"

Taking my notepad and writing down
the *lies,* r*acial comments, control, lies*
about the Holy Spirit and healing, etc.

Convinced of all the wrong teachings,
I had to ask **God** to *help* me forgive.

Mark 11:25: *"And when ye stand praying, forgive, if ye have ought against any, that your Father also, which is in Heaven, may forgive you your trespasses."*

Chapter 7

No More Being a Castaway From ______!

I regretted believing the past lies of Satan, that I was a castaway in family, in marriages, in homes, churches, jobs, and friendships.

Never truly knowing who I was in Christ!

My question to you, as you listen and read: "Could my lifetime of scars from my pain, cause you to reach to Jesus, changing your life?

In God's grace and mercy, He has re-written my life!

Believing now, through this lifetime journey, that **God** loves me, provides for me, protects me, prospers me, in ways that bring me to daily praise and thanksgiving!

Because of faith, I truly have a *Godly love* and reverence. Prompted by faith, daily having a relationship with the **Holy Spirit,** *urged on by faith,* choosing to follow **Jesus**!

Just as I read years ago, in 1998,
with my dad, my Pastor now.

To become a follower of ***Jesus!***

John 21:19: "Follow me."

This book was a journey through some painful seasons of my life, to a *life of restoration* of what was taken from me.

Is there, in your life's journey, a place that you too have been a castaway?

Chapter 8

Seeking the Lord

Rose and I went to church on a Saturday night, for prayer time about the upcoming camp meeting at the church.

We agreed in prayer, "*Lord, who do you want in the pulpit in this camp meeting?*" for there was one night that was still not confirmed.

That Wednesday night of the camp meeting, the guest speaker was singing to the Holy Spirit and gave a book to me.

As I received the book, in my spirit came: *"YOUR MIRACLE IS IN YOUR HANDS!"*

Mal 3:10: "*Bring ye all the tithes into the storehouse, that there may be meat in mine house, and prove me now herewith, saith the Lord of host. If I will not open you the windows of heaven, and pour you out a blessing, that there shall not be room enough to receive it.*"

I shared my prayer with Rose and her
husband, praying in agreement, that God
would make a way to go to the Benny Hinn
crusade coming to Oklahoma City, OK

We waited with *expectation,* for there was
nothing else that we could do.

The man that I had broken the demonic
soul-ties with, asked Rose's husband,
"How much is needed for the trip?"

—Reaching in his wallet, giving
the money for the trip!

We agreed to give a Thanksgiving
offering at the crusade, for we knew
that God had answered our prayers!

As we traveled, we were able to go through
a drive-through for our supper and received
a good parking place at the crusade.

I experienced worship through a new level of thanksgiving.

As Benny Hinn began to speak, he stopped and said, "The Holy Spirit does not need me tonight."

He instructed us to line up and come walking by the podium if we needed something from the Lord. Then he sat back down.

We were there until after12:00 midnight, with the praise music still playing. Benny Hinn had left at about 10:00 pm.

As it was my turn to walk across by the podium, I experienced the *gift of love* and *healing in my heart!*

.

Chapter 9

Reaching for something I have never had

One of the coldest days in Jan', in the 90s,
I chose to go to a women's crisis center,
while living in a small run-down trailer.

Uncontrollable anger was rising in me.

I had packed a small suitcase, under the bed, as instructed, with the phone number and quarters for the payphone that I had to walk to.

Waiting in the cold, at the payphone
for the cab, I knew it was the hardest
decision I had ever made.

I knew I was not coming back, and my
feelings became numb. I was walking away
from *home* and *2 dogs*, and *everything I knew.*

After the crisis center staff showed me a bed,

I knelt beside the bed, crying out to **God** for help!

I wanted to change. I knew I had made so many mistakes

and did not know how to fix them!

I was later connected to Gloria, an Independent *Mary Kay Consultant,* and she came to pick me up, getting my hair trimmed and colored, and having a Mary Kay facial.

Sunday morning, Rose picked me up for *church.*

Our *guest speaker was from Oral Roberts University.* He spoke, "T**here is someone here today that is at a crossroad and needs to decide right now!"**

Reading Mark 12:30: *"And thou shalt love the Lord thy God with all thy heart, and with all thy soul, and with all thy mind, and with all thy strength. This is the first commandment."*

I started to cry, for I knew, right at that moment, ***God*** *was speaking to me!*

In my spirit, I said, "Yes Lord!"

Then the speaker said, *"Now that you have made your choice,* for this is the first, and most important of all decisions, in *following me!"*

Months later, I came across Gloria's Mary Kay business card that I received at the women's crisis center, with all the Mary Kay samples!

That year at Christmas, Gloria surprised me with the whole skincare kit of everything I needed.

We had Christmas lunch. I was compelled to give back to women, by being an Independent Mary Kay Consultant, blessing each wounded woman, meeting them in crisis centers and different women's groups.

I was confronted with why I wanted to wear make-up, in one of my Family Life Skills classes. I carried my emotional pain in my face and eyes, that I did not want anyone to see.

After a while I saw my eyes change, from dark to bright blue, no *more hiding behind the make-up!*

I have a new understanding of wearing my make-up, as it has become a lifestyle of different colors to compliment me. Now, having a new love and compassion by being an Independent Mary Kay Consultant

To enhance women's Godly beauty in each woman I meet!

How can I pray for you?

Send your prayer request to:

brooksb_castaway38@yahoo.com

I would like to invite you to be a partner with me in publishing more of these books and others.

Using this opportunity, by placing a Mary Kay order through my web page:

http://www.marykay.com/bbrooks8184

I will be sending a special email to each partner, with how my books have touched the lives of others just like you.

Contact me:

www.facebook.com/consultantBrooksBarbaraAnn

www.twitter.com/consultant@BarbaraABrook1

www.instagram.com/customerbarbarabrooks4

BarbaraAnnBrooks.com

www.ingramcontent.com/pod-product-compliance
Lightning Source LLC
Chambersburg PA
CBHW031541040426
42445CB00010B/645
* 9 7 8 0 5 7 8 9 2 8 4 9 4 *